●═ Continuoul Process Improvement

A Practical Guide To Improving Processes For Measurable Results

Richard Y. Chang

KOGAN PAGE

First published in 1993 by Richard Chang Associates, Inc., USA.

This edition published in 1995 by Kogan Page Ltd.

Kogan Page Limited
120 Pentonville Road
London N1 9JN

© 1993, Richard Chang Associates, Inc., 41 Corporate Park, Suite 230, Irvine, CA 92714 USA.

British Library Cataloguing in Publication Data

A CIP record for this book is available from the British Library.

ISBN 0 7494 1652 1

Printed and bound in Great Britain by
Biddles Ltd, Guildford and King's Lynn

ACKNOWLEDGMENTS

About The Author

Richard Y. Chang is President and CEO of Richard Chang Associates, Inc., a diversified organizational improvement consulting firm based in Irvine, California. He is internationally recognized for his management strategy, quality improvement, organization development, customer satisfaction, and human resource development expertise.

The author would like to acknowledge the support of the entire team of professionals at Richard Chang Associates, Inc. for their contribution to the guidebook development process. In addition, special thanks are extended to the many client organizations who have helped us shape the practical ideas and proven methods shared in this guidebook.

Additional Credits

Editors:	Sarah Ortlieb Fraser and Ruth Stingley
Reviewers:	Jean Lucas, Jim Greeley, and Dottie Snyder
Graphic Layout:	Christina Slater
Cover Design:	John Odam Design Associates

PREFACE

The 1990's have already presented individuals and organizations with some very difficult challenges to face and overcome. So who will have the advantage as we move toward the year 2000 and beyond?

The advantage will belong to those with a commitment to continuous learning. Whether on an individual basis or as an entire organization, one key ingredient to building a continuous learning environment is *The Practical Guidebook Collection* brought to you by the Publications Division of Richard Chang Associates, Inc.

After understanding the future *"learning needs"* expressed by our clients and other potential customers, we are pleased to publish *The Practical Guidebook Collection*. These guidebooks are designed to provide you with proven, *"real-world"* tips, tools, and techniques— on a wide range of subjects—that you can apply in the workplace and/or on a personal level immediately.

Once you've had a chance to benefit from *The Practical Guidebook Collection*, please share your feedback with us. We've included a brief *Evaluation and Feedback Form* at the end of the guidebook that you can fax to us.

With your feedback, we can continuously improve the resources we are providing through the Publications Division of Richard Chang Associates, Inc.

Wishing you successful reading,

Richard Y. Chang
President and CEO
Richard Chang Associates, Inc.

TABLE OF CONTENTS

"We must not stay as we are, doing always what was done last time, or we shall stick in the mud."

George Bernard Shaw

CHAPTER ONE

INTRODUCTION

Lewis Carroll once wrote, *"If you don't care where you're going, any road will take you there."* But if you do care where you're going, then you need to discover and travel the right road. There is a method for helping you find that road to quality improvement and successfully transporting you down it toward your goals. The method is Continuous Process Improvement (CPI).

CPI is not mysterious or complicated. Applying the specific philosophy and techniques of CPI requires only two things:

1. A desire to improve your current business or personal processes and produce more successful results.

2. A willingness to take the necessary steps to accomplish your improvement goals.

Why Read This Guidebook?

That's the same as asking, *"Why bother to improve?"* We must constantly improve because the world is changing daily. We are becoming a more knowledgeable and competitive global community. If you don't strive to improve quality and productivity, you may find that one day your opportunities will shrink and the rest of the world is passing you by. CPI philosophy and techniques will not only ensure your ability to compete for world-class performance, but will even help you pull ahead of the competition.

According to business research, poor quality can cost organizations 20 to 25 percent of their gross revenues. That much loss can be disastrous to organizations operating in today's competitive environment. CPI can help you and your organization work together to produce and maintain the kind of quality you need to avoid such loss. Continuous process improvement has become the key business requirement for the 1990s and beyond.

The only way you can remain successful is by continually improving your way of doing things and surpassing your goals and achievements. It goes beyond outside competition. You need to compete with yourself—always striving to do your personal best and achieve greater excellence.

The same holds true for organizations and companies. If you wait until a competitor is surpassing you or shining a glaring light on your productivity and quality flaws, then you're already at a disadvantage. CPI enables you and your organization to act on an internal motivation to improve instead of react to an external condition that suddenly demands it.

This book shows you how to use CPI techniques to improve business or personal processes and consequently, their results. Don't be fooled by the myth that just because a process has worked well in the past, there's no need to improve it. Needs and demands are constantly changing and so must the methods for meeting them. You can't stop progress. You just need to make certain that you're always a part of it.

Who Is It For?

This guidebook is for individuals and small groups working on CPI and self-managed *(or related)* teams. The examples, case study, and scenarios that follow focus on a service-related process in a product-oriented business setting. However, you can easily apply CPI concepts, techniques, and methods to other situations, such as personal arenas, service-oriented businesses, community groups, government agencies, education, manufacturing, and nonprofit organizations.

When And How To Use It

You can use this guidebook as a step-by-step guide for applying a systematic CPI methodology on the job or in personal situations. It will help you understand how to plan and implement a CPI project effectively.

The CPI method presented in this book really works. By learning and practicing its techniques, you will soon become an old hand at the method and a fan of it as well. You will be amazed at the positive results process improvements will bring to both your personal and business lives.

The first time you attempt to improve a process, you should carefully follow each step of the five-phase model presented in this guidebook. In the future, you may find yourself sailing through some steps and focusing more on other steps.

In addition, you will find worksheets and/or planning tools at the end of the chapters. Please use them to practice some of the CPI ideas and techniques.

WHAT IS CPI?

*"Be methodical if you would succeed in business or anything.
Method is essential if you would get through your work easily and
with economy of time."*

William Matthews

CPI is a systematic approach that you can use to make incremental
and breakthrough improvements in processes that produce
products and services for customers. By utilizing CPI, you take a
detailed look at processes and discover ways to improve them.
Your end result is a faster, better, more efficient, or cost-effective
way to produce a product or service.

Let's zero in on the core concepts and definitions of CPI. Our focus
is on CPI concepts and benefits relating to your workplace, but
keep in mind that you can successfully apply CPI methods to your
personal life as well.

To understand how CPI works, you need to know what a *process* is
and analyze its components.

What Is A Process?

Almost everything you do in your daily personal and professional life is a process. For example, you might:

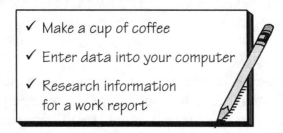

✓ Make a cup of coffee

✓ Enter data into your computer

✓ Research information for a work report

Whether you are performing common actions such as these, or carrying out more complex tasks, such as calculating the origins of the universe, you are participating in some type of process.

Simply speaking, a process is:

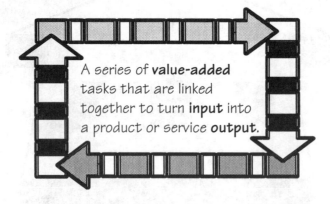

A series of **value-added** tasks that are linked together to turn **input** into a product or service **output**.

Key Process Terms

Let's look at some of the terms used in the definition of a process.

Value-added versus non value-added tasks

A value-added task is an essential work effort (*i.e., it contributes to your ability to produce a process output*).

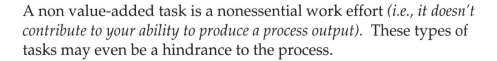

A non value-added task is a nonessential work effort (*i.e., it doesn't contribute to your ability to produce a process output*). These types of tasks may even be a hindrance to the process.

Input And Output

Input is the information, materials, and resources you need to create products or services. It is the starting point of the production process.

Output is the product, information, or service you provide to another individual or work group. It is the end point *(or result)* of the process.

The points where a process starts *(input)* and ends *(output)* are the process boundaries.

Here are two examples of these concepts:

	PROCESS EXAMPLES	
	MAKING COFFEE	ENTERING COMPUTER DATA
INPUT	Coffee, water, filter, measuring device, coffee maker, cup	Research information, raw data
VALUE-ADDED TASKS	⇒ Insert filter ⇒ Measure and add coffee ⇒ Measure and add water ⇒ Turn on coffee maker ⇒ Pour coffee into cup	⇒ Turn on computer ⇒ Use keyboard to enter data ⇒ Save data ⇒ Print data
NON VALUE-ADDED TASKS	⇒ Measure the coffee grain by grain ⇒ Draw designs on filter ⇒ Move coffee maker from counter to counter	⇒ Provide extra graphs and illustrations ⇒ Translate data into several different computer languages ⇒ Put colored cellophane over monitor
OUTPUT	Cup of coffee	Printout of data

Understanding The Process Chain

The Supplier-Producer-Customer chain is the heartbeat of any process relationship. Each link in the Supplier-Producer-Customer chain is interrelated and interdependent.

Here is a step-by-step illustration of the Supplier-Producer-Customer chain:

Value-Added Process

❶ Everyone plays a role

❷ Requirements drive the relationship

❸ Producer processes are bounded by inputs and outputs

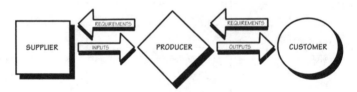

❹ Feedback is the key to continuous improvement

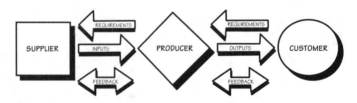

Let's explore the role each element of the Supplier-Producer-Customer chain plays in the process of making coffee.

Supplier

You can't make coffee without coffee grains—the input. A supplier must furnish the input according to the requirements of the producer. In this case, the supplier of coffee-making products might be a store.

Producer

The producer makes the coffee. Because the producer is responsible for the operation of the process, the producer is also known as the process owner. A producer is any individual, work group, or department that ensures the smooth and effective operation of a process. The producer provides output according to the requirements of the customers of the process.

Customer

The customer will drink that freshly brewed cup of coffee. The customer is any person, work group, or department that receives the process output. The customer defines the requirements for the output created by and received from the producer. There are basically two kinds of customers:

A. The internal customer

The internal customer is an individual, work group, or department that works for the same organization as the producer. For example, you might enter computer data for your company's payroll department *(the internal customer)*.

B. The external customer

The external customer is an individual, work group, or department that does not work for the same organization as the producer. For example, if you ran a coffee bistro, you might brew some exotic coffee for a paying *(external)* customer.

Focusing On Process Requirements

⟹ Requirements fuel the Supplier-Producer-Customer relationship.

⟹ All requirements are Customer-driven.

⟹ Producer requirements must be fulfilled by the Supplier so that the Producer can satisfy his/her Customers' requirements.

Customer requirements are essentially the needs and expectations of the customer.

What is the difference between needs and expectations? Let's look at coffee again. Suppose a customer *(Aaron)* has arrived at your office and wants a cup of coffee. You escort him to the coffee machine and pour him a cup. Aaron takes one sip of the coffee and says, *"Yuk, what do you call this?"* And you sputter, *"Coffee . . . I thought you said you needed coffee."* He replies, *"I do need coffee, but I also expect it to be hot and strong, not lukewarm and weak!"*

Aaron got what he *needed,* but not what he *expected.*

Here's another example. Maria is the department manager at a pharmaceutical company. It's her responsibility to prepare a weekly inventory report regarding all the company's vitamin supplies. As the producer or process owner of that report, Maria has to confirm the report requirements *(needs and expectations)* with her customer. Maria has two key customers—her immediate boss *(the department manager)* and the company's senior management team. The requirements of her key customers are in conflict. Whose requirements should she follow?

In this case, she should focus on the requirements of the senior management team, since they are the primary customers for the report. After discussing it with team members, Maria determined that they had the following requirements for the inventory report.

NEED		EXPECTATION
A weekly inventory report	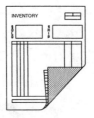	• Accurate • Neat • Double-spaced • No more than five pages long
Information on multivitamin formulas separated from information on individual vitamin supplements	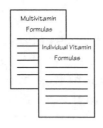	• Alphabetical order for each category
Report delivered each Friday		• Delivered by 10 a.m.
Sealed report		• Report delivered in an envelope and marked *"confidential"* with a seal

Continual Feedback Is Vital

Because every process is customer-driven, it is important to communicate with your customers to see if you are meeting their requirements, or if their requirements have changed. This dialogue needs to be an ongoing event. You can actually measure your success by improvements in customer satisfaction.

In addition, it's important that you incorporate continual feedback and measurement between Customers-Producers and Producers-Suppliers at various process stages.

Don't wait for feedback to come to you. Actively solicit it from your customers by asking questions, gathering data, and taking surveys. You cannot determine or update process requirements without measuring the quality and effectiveness of your output.

Don't assume that you know your customers' needs and expectations. Since those requirements can change regularly, feedback is the primary ingredient of that measurement. Before instituting a new process or changing an existing one, get feedback from your customers. If you don't, you can waste a lot of time, energy, and money making unnecessary changes.

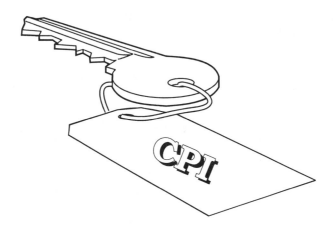

CPI Is The Key To Success

CPI is a practical and powerful tool that can help you successfully promote and maintain quality in your workplace and personal life. By fully understanding the impacts and consequences of your activities, you can determine if your way of doing things is the best way to serve your customers and organization.

The concepts presented in this chapter are the basic elements of CPI. The following chapters show a simple, systematic approach that you can use to improve your processes and to meet changing quality demands as well as customer satisfaction requirements.

CHAPTER TWO WORKSHEET:
GETTING ACQUAINTED WITH CPI

Use this worksheet to understand some of the processes you currently implement.

1. List below the primary Supplier-Producer-Customer chains that you are part of in your workplace and/or your personal life.

PRIMARY SUPPLIERS AND INPUTS	PRODUCER	PRIMARY CUSTOMERS AND OUTPUTS
(From Whom and What)	*(Your Value-Added Process)*	*(To Whom and What)*
Suppliers: Inputs:	Process:	Customers: Outputs:
Suppliers: Inputs:	Process:	Customers: Outputs:
Suppliers: Inputs:	Process:	Customers: Outputs:

2. List below one of your key work processes that most impacts the quality of outputs for your primary customers. Make a brief list of the value-added and non value-added tasks that are currently involved in the process.

Process: _____

VALUE-ADDED TASKS	NON VALUE-ADDED TASKS

Note: If you are unsure whether an activity is value-added or not, list it under one of the columns and circle it *(or put a check mark near it for future reference).*

3. Select one of the non value-added tasks listed above and identify some possible causes, as well as ways you might be able to reduce or eliminate this task.

NON VALUE-ADDED TASK	POSSIBLE CAUSES	WAYS TO REDUCE OR ELIMINATE

APPLYING A SYSTEMATIC CPI MODEL

"The message from the moon . . . is that no problem need any longer be considered insoluble."

Norman Cousins

Continuous process improvement isn't a one-time investment. If your goal is to achieve total customer satisfaction, both internally and externally, CPI must become an ongoing affair, a way of life.

But how do you reach that point? You must learn how to implement CPI in a systematic fashion. Once this approach becomes ingrained, you'll find that CPI doesn't require methodical, conscious application. It'll become like second nature to you.

The SAMIE Model

One very workable approach to CPI is the SAMIE Model. The term SAMIE is an acronym for Select, Analyze, Measure, Improve, Evaluate. Each phase of the SAMIE model consists of steps that will guide you through a CPI cycle. Of course, you can adapt the SAMIE model to suit your own improvement efforts and organizational requirements.

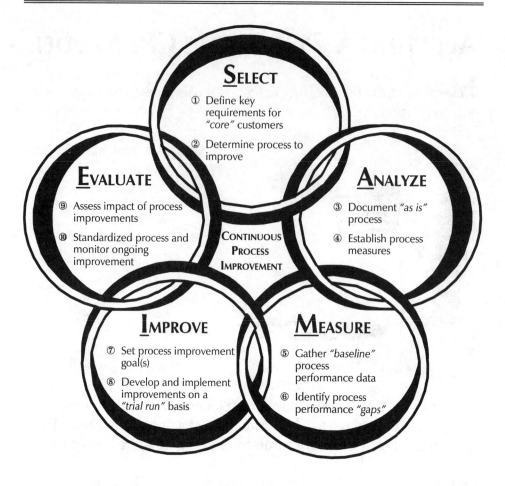

As you pursue CPI using the SAMIE model, you might discover that some of the major steps overlap. You might even find that you don't have to follow every step in detail. For example, if you already know the process that you need to improve, you may spend less time on the steps in the Select phase and quickly move on to the steps in the Analyze phase.

There might be times when you have to retrace your steps back to square one. For example, you could be in the midst of documenting a process and learn that you need to go back and redefine your customer's output requirements before continuing the Analyze phase.

The SAMIE model helps you stay focused, avoid pitfalls, and save valuable time and energy as you and/or your improvement team pursue CPI. Before long, you'll not only use it to fix troubled areas, but you'll also use it to reach greater heights of excellence in already productive processes. There's no end to what CPI can do for your company.

CHAPTER FOUR

ONE COMPANY'S APPROACH TO CPI

Case Example: Sure Strike Bowling, Inc.

Sure Strike Bowling, Inc., a bowling ball and equipment company, desired customer satisfaction above all else. Their company motto is: *"Our customer is our kingpin!"* Sure Strike was continually striving to improve customer satisfaction by producing quality merchandise and service. But employees felt they could still improve internal operations.

The sales force was especially interested in improving customer satisfaction. The sales people spent the most time with Sure Strike's external customers. If the customers were consistently satisfied with Sure Strike's products and services, then the sales force would have an easier time selling merchandise.

Sure Strike hired an outside consulting firm to conduct a customer satisfaction survey. After analyzing the data, Sure Strike determined that *"timely returns and exchanges of merchandise"* was of primary concern to core customers.

Executive management and the sales force held independent meetings to discuss this information. Although they spent a great deal of time and energy, neither of these groups was able to identify the processes that needed improvement. And from past experience, management knew that if they didn't take the time to fully understand the situation and target the right processes, making the correct improvements would occur in a *"hit or miss"* fashion.

Management decided to take a proactive approach to the improvement effort. They created a six-member cross-functional team *(they chose each team member from a different internal functional area)*. Since each team member came from a department that performed related, yet different processes, each member brought a unique perspective to the team. They hoped their combined knowledge and input would result in success. Their goal was to improve the processes involved in returning and exchanging merchandise. The team needed to do the following:

Understand core customer requirements

Select the first process to improve and processes to improve later

Analyze and improve the process

Establish measurement methods to monitor and continuously improve the process

The six team members were:

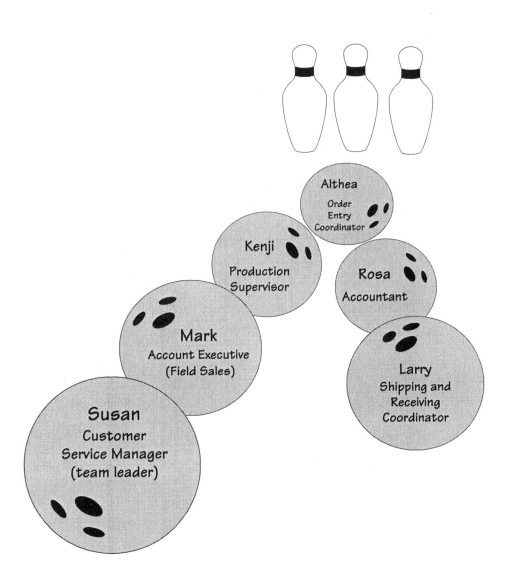

PHASE ONE: SELECT

If you select the wrong process to improve, any improvements you make in that process may not add value or might be meaningless. Take, for example, a department store's attempt to increase customer satisfaction by changing the way salespeople handle transactions. If customers have no complaint with that process, the *"improvement"* may not help the company reach its goal of increasing customer satisfaction.

In general, any process you choose to improve should be:

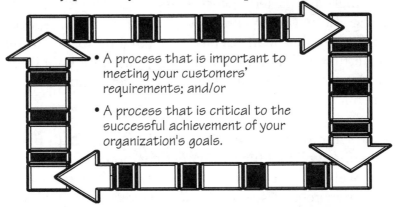

- A process that is important to meeting your customers' requirements; and/or
- A process that is critical to the successful achievement of your organization's goals.

Selecting the right process to improve involves the following two major steps:

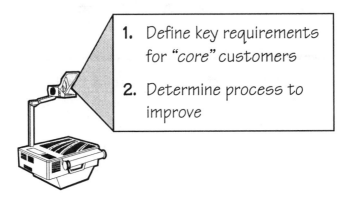

1. Define key requirements for "core" customers

2. Determine process to improve

Watch as Sure Strike's team carried out these major steps and key activities to select a process to improve.

1. Define Key Requirements For "Core" Customers

If customer satisfaction is your goal, you must understand what your direct customers require of you. Ask them what they want you to do or provide, and then use this feedback to focus on process improvements. Doing so will increase customer satisfaction levels.

However, you can't define key requirements unless you know who your customers are. External customers are easy to identify, but pinpointing internal customers may be more complex, especially if your organization has many departments that perform interrelated tasks. Your first item of business involves targeting your internal and external customers. Only then can you determine their key requirements.

Sure Strike's improvement team was ready to begin. It's first task was to identify which of the company's core internal and external customers were involved in and directly affected by returns and exchanges of merchandise *(the identified improvement opportunity area)*. Susan, the team leader, got the ball rolling. She named the Customer Service Department and External Buying Customer as core customers. Soon everyone began brainstorming core customer groups, and Larry recorded them on a flip chart:

- Customer Service Department
- External Buying Customer
- Sales Department
- Executive Management Team
- Packing/ShippingDepartment
- AccountingDepartment
- Order Department
- Production Department
- Purchasing Department
- Warehouse
- Billing/Accounts
- Receivable Department
- Design/Engineering Department

The team then ranked the customer category list according to which customer was most important to satisfy. The most important customer would become its top priority, and that customer turned out to be the external buying customer.

The team continued by brainstorming a more specific list of external customers to narrow the focus of the category. Larry listed the external customers on a flip chart. The list included:

- Sporting Goods Stores
- Department Stores
- Bowling Pro Shops
- Bowling Centers
- Multipurpose Recreation Centers
- Military Bases
- TV Game Shows
- Individual Buyers
- Other Sporting Equipment Manufacturers

The team then ranked the list of external buying customers according to priority. The team based its decisions on such criteria as: buying volume, potential for returns and exchanges, and frequency of customer contact.

The top three external buying customers most affected by Sure Strike's return and exchange processes were:

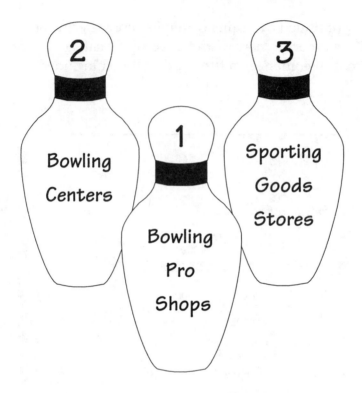

The team's next task was to determine the customers' requirements regarding the company's return and exchange processes. Larry reminded the group that when it came to customer requirements, they needed a full understanding of the customers' needs and expectations. *"For example,"* he explained, *"it's not enough that my department packs the bowling balls carefully in easy-to-open boxes—most of the customers expect that the different weights will be clearly marked on the outside of the boxes in the designated spot."*

Understanding customer requirements

Customers, both internal and external, dictate how you carry out your job responsibilities. If you are inefficient and inept, you'll hear about it from your customers. Likewise, if you are exceptional, it'll show in their response to you and your product or service. Exceptional producers know what their customers require and then meet or exceed those requirements.

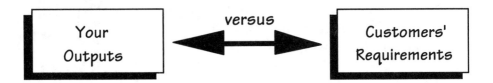

☞ This is what you produce. The output can be a product or service, and customer satisfaction depends on whether the output meets the customers' requirements.	☞ Requirements are what the customer *needs* and/or *expects* from the output you produce. They should be very specific, and related directly from the customer.

Customer requirements typically fall into some of the following areas:

SAMPLE CUSTOMER REQUIREMENT AREAS			
⇒	*Timeliness*	⇒	*Quantity*
⇒	*Cost*	⇒	*Thoroughness*
⇒	*Accuracy*	⇒	*Dimension*
⇒	*Functionality*	⇒	*Yield*
⇒	*Responsiveness*	⇒	*Price*
⇒	*Follow-through*	⇒	*Availability*

To define and confirm your customers' requirements, follow these three basic substeps:

❶ Identify your customers' requirement areas

Brainstorm the requirement areas you believe to be important to the customer. These requirement areas will generally fall into one or more categories *(e.g., timeliness, quantity, cost, etc.)*. After verifying these areas with your customer, you can identify specific requirements.

❷ Develop interview/survey questions

Customer Requirement Area	Interview Questions	Importance Low High
		1 2 3 4 5 6 7 8 9 10
		1 2 3 4 5 6 7 8 9 10
		1 2 3 4 5 6 7 8 9 10
		1 2 3 4 5 6 7 8 9 10
		1 2 3 4 5 6 7 8 9 10
		1 2 3 4 5 6 7 8 9 10

You may use a short list of questions or a questionnaire survey. It should elicit the feedback needed to determine whether customer requirements are being met and to establish the importance of a particular requirement.

❸ Interview/survey your customer

Whenever possible, interview your customer in a face-to-face meeting. Write down all feedback so you and/or your team can review it later. When defining customer requirements, be sure to understand both needs and expectations.

Identify your customers' requirement areas

Identifying your customers' requirement areas from their point of view helps you stay focused on critical improvement opportunities. Put yourself in your customers' shoes and visualize what they might require. Are they primarily interested in saving money? Time? Or perhaps they'd like you to offer a wider variety of goods and services?

Sure Strike's improvement team brainstormed a list of potential customer requirement areas. Having dealt directly with Sure Strike's external customers, Susan and Mark had some valuable insight into customer requirements. The team members themselves were internal customers of the return and exchange processes! They believed that when a customer was returning or exchanging merchandise, the primary customer requirement areas included:

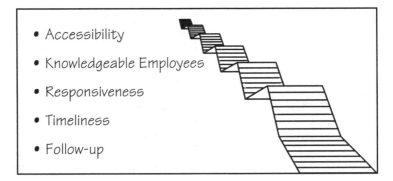

- Accessibility
- Knowledgeable Employees
- Responsiveness
- Timeliness
- Follow-up

The team realized that these were broad areas of customer requirements. However, they knew that when Kenji, Althea, and Rosa interviewed selected representatives from the core customer segments, they would learn the customers' specific needs and expectations. For example, they'd find out how quickly customers expected to receive refund checks or credit to their accounts.

The survey sheet and face-to-face customer interviews would also provide them with more well-defined information about their customers' key requirements.

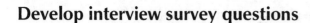

Develop interview survey questions

Once you've identified your customers' requirement areas, you can formulate interview/survey questions that relate to those areas. Devise questions that will help you gauge where improvements are needed. Also, make your questionnaire short; your customers need to know that you consider their time valuable.

The Sure Strike team developed a questionnaire to help determine specifics about each of the primary requirement areas. Here's a sample of the survey sheet they created:

Customer Requirement Area	Specific Expectations (comments)	Satisfaction Rating (circle one)	Importance Scale (circle one)
TIMELINESS (e.g., number of days for refund or credit)	A.	1 2 3 4 5 6 7 8 9 10	1 2 3 4 5 6 7 8 9 10
	B.	1 2 3 4 5 6 7 8 9 10	1 2 3 4 5 6 7 8 9 10
	C.	1 2 3 4 5 6 7 8 9 10	1 2 3 4 5 6 7 8 9 10
RESPONSIVENESS (e.g., thoroughness of assistance provided)	A.	1 2 3 4 5 6 7 8 9 10	1 2 3 4 5 6 7 8 9 10
	B.	1 2 3 4 5 6 7 8 9 10	1 2 3 4 5 6 7 8 9 10
	C.	1 2 3 4 5 6 7 8 9 10	1 2 3 4 5 6 7 8 9 10
FOLLOW-UP (e.g., dependability to provide answers to questions)	A.	1 2 3 4 5 6 7 8 9 10	1 2 3 4 5 6 7 8 9 10
	B.	1 2 3 4 5 6 7 8 9 10	1 2 3 4 5 6 7 8 9 10
	C.	1 2 3 4 5 6 7 8 9 10	1 2 3 4 5 6 7 8 9 10
ACCESSIBILITY (e.g., ability to reach each person on first try)	A.	1 2 3 4 5 6 7 8 9 10	1 2 3 4 5 6 7 8 9 10
	B.	1 2 3 4 5 6 7 8 9 10	1 2 3 4 5 6 7 8 9 10
	C.	1 2 3 4 5 6 7 8 9 10	1 2 3 4 5 6 7 8 9 10
KNOWLEDGEABLE EMPLOYEES (e.g., ability to answer all relevant questions)	A.	1 2 3 4 5 6 7 8 9 10	1 2 3 4 5 6 7 8 9 10
	B.	1 2 3 4 5 6 7 8 9 10	1 2 3 4 5 6 7 8 9 10
	C.	1 2 3 4 5 6 7 8 9 10	1 2 3 4 5 6 7 8 9 10

Interview/survey your customer

The final substep in defining key requirements for core customers is to interview your customers. Doing so will enable you to key in on their needs and expectations; then, and only then, can you target which processes to improve.

Kenji, Althea, and Rosa used the survey sheet the team had developed as a guide for their face-to-face customer interviews. They made appointments with some external customers, arranging to meet them at their places of business.

The customers were happy to cooperate. Mark and Susan discovered that they were pleased by Sure Strike's interest in getting their feedback, and the interviews proved to be very informative. An unexpected benefit of the interviews was great public relations for the company.

Customer requirements feedback

After you've completed all of the customer interviews, you need to make sense of the data you've gathered. Which requirement area is most important? Which area needs the most work? Customer feedback is valuable information; use it to your advantage.

It took three weeks for the team members to gather all the requirement data regarding returns and exchanges from the external customers. When the team met again, the members shared the requirement data and listed it on their flip chart. They learned that the customers most often expressed the following requirements *(needs and expectations):*

- ➧ Refund or credit to account mailed within 72 hours of receipt of returned merchandise
- ➧ Shipment of exchanged merchandise within 72 hours of receipt of merchandised to be exchanged
- ➧ Efficient handling of customer telephone inquires
- ➧ Correct amount of money refunded (or credited to account) in accordance with refund policy
- ➧ Receive quality merchandise when exchanging unsatisfactory merchandise
- ➧ Exchange unsold merchandise (in resaleable condition) for other merchandise of comparable value
- ➧ Receive follow-up confirmation of action being taken within 24 hours of receipt of returned merchandise if return will not be resolved and mailed within 72 hours
- ➧ Have merchandise warranties go into effect automatically following purchase without paperwork

2. Determine Process To Improve

Now that you're aware of your customers' requirements, you're ready to pinpoint which process to improve. Selecting the right process is crucial to your success, and it involves four basic substeps:

➢ List relevant processes that affect customer satisfaction

➢ Establish selection criteria

➢ Identify relationship between criteria and process

➢ Prioritize and select a process for improvement

Following these four substeps will ensure that your improvement efforts are focused on the correct process.

List relevant processes that affect customer satisfaction

Together with your work group or process improvement team, brainstorm a list of work processes that relate to problem areas (*improvement opportunities*) in meeting customer requirements. Your list may have anywhere from two to six or more processes. Make sure these processes have clear boundaries; they must have a definite starting and stopping point. Also, check to see if your process is in fact a process or subprocess, not a higher level system (*like the entire Accounting system*) or a specific individual task.

The members of Sure Strike's improvement team looked at the results of its customer assessment and agreed that the majority of the requirements focused on the timely resolution of returns and exchanges. Rosa suggested that the team members brainstorm a list of company processes that related to the customer-defined return and exchange requirements. Their brainstorming produced the following list:

- Merchandise Return Process
- Cash Refund Process
- Account Credit Refund Process
- Customer Complaint Handling Process
- Accounts Payable Process
- Accounts Receivable Process
- Merchandise Distribution Process
- Customer Order Data Entry Process
- Merchandise Exchange Process
- Customer Confirmation Process

Following additional discussion, the team decided that the most critical and relevant processes that addressed customer requirements were the:

➠ Merchandise Return Process
➠ Cash Refund Process
➠ Customer Complaint Handling Process

Establish selection criteria

After you've completed your list of potential processes, brainstorm a list of criteria for your process selection. Your criteria might include such factors as the level of control you have, the time involved, the cost and resource requirements, and the probability of success. These criteria will shape your idea of which process you should attempt to improve first.

Sure Strike's CPI team knew it could not improve all of the listed processes at one time. The team members would have to initially target just one of the processes. Kenji suggested that they establish some process selection criteria to help them rate the processes. That way, they'd be able to select the process that customers felt required improvement and that they could undertake successfully.

They would then try to improve that process by applying the SAMIE model. The group came up with the following process selection criteria for their particular situation:

✔ Customer dissatisfaction with the current process
✔ Control over improving the process
✔ Importance to the customer
✔ Ability to improve with existing resources
✔ Benefit for improving the process
✔ Probability of success

Identify relationship between criteria and process

It's at this point that you take your list of work processes and rate them against the selection criteria you chose. A Selection Matrix is a useful tool for this step. Rate each work process on a scale of one to ten, with one as the lowest score, and ten as the highest.

Using the team's process selection criteria, Rosa volunteered to create a Process Selection Matrix to help decide which process to work on first. Here's what it looked like:

	RELEVANT WORK PROCESSES		
SELECTION CRITERIA	**PROCESS #1** Merchandise Return Process	**PROCESS #2** Cash Refund Process	**PROCESS #3** Customer Complaint Handling Process
Customer dissatisfaction with the current process	4	8	4
Control over improving the process	6	10	8
Importance to the customer	10	10	8
Ability to improve with existing resources	6	9	5
Benefit for improving the process	8	7	9
Probability of success	7	9	8
Total points	41	53	42

Prioritize and select a process for improvement

Add up the points for each process, and identify the process with the highest score. This is the process you may want to improve first. If your top contender is a close call, you and your improvement team may want to rate the top processes again since one member's perception of a criterion may be different from that of another member.

After rating each of the processes according to its criteria, the team decided that the *Cash Refund Process* was its highest priority process to improve. The team believed that by improving this process, the company's external customers would feel that Sure Strike was sensitive to their monetary needs and expectations. And improving this process would also help project a customer-friendly image that could attract even more customers.

Susan suggested that at their next meeting they should begin analyzing the cash refund process.

Selecting the appropriate process to improve is essential to any successful CPI endeavor. It ensures that you're running in the right direction. That's necessary if you want to win the race to gain customer satisfaction.

CHAPTER FIVE WORKSHEET:
IDENTIFYING CORE CUSTOMER SEGMENTS
AND THEIR KEY REQUIREMENTS

List key customer requirements for two professional and/or personal processes. Then list how you determined those requirements *(e.g., through conversations with the customer, third-party observations, your personal opinion based on experience with the customer, etc.).* Check to see if you understand the requirements from the customers' point of view.

CORE CUSTOMER SEGMENT #1:	
KEY CUSTOMER REQUIREMENTS	**HOW KEY REQUIREMENTS DETERMINED**
A.	
B.	
C.	
D.	
E.	

CORE CUSTOMER SEGMENT #2:	
KEY CUSTOMER REQUIREMENTS	**HOW KEY REQUIREMENTS DETERMINED**
A.	
B.	
C.	
D.	
E.	

PHASE TWO: ANALYZE

You now know which process you must improve to increase customer satisfaction. But improvement isn't an automatic given. Unless you understand how the process currently works, you won't be able to determine how to improve it. The first thing you must do is analyze the process.

Analyzing the process involves the following two major steps:

3. Document "as is" process

4. Establish process measures

3. Document "As Is" Process

During this first step in phase two, you'll need to define and map out all the activities involved in your chosen process. This will provide you with a clear overview of the process and allow you to determine if some of the activities are non value-added. There are two basic substeps for documenting a process:

SUBSTEP	TECHNIQUE	DESCRIPTION
A. List the major process tasks	Process Tasks	List the major tasks and decisions required to translate inputs into outputs.
B. Create a process flow chart		Create a visual diagram of how the process currently works. Use it as an ongoing working document.

A. List the major process tasks

Documenting the process involves identifying the major tasks of the process you have selected. Specifically, this includes:

1. Defining the input and output involved in the process.

2. Listing the six to ten major tasks that get you from the supplier inputs to the producer outputs.

3. Identifying the smaller subtasks and decisions that link the major tasks together.

Sure Strike's CPI team wanted to make certain that it could produce a complete list of the major tasks and decision points. Larry suggested that the team members ask questions as they worked through the process. They came up with the following questions to guide them in listing the tasks.

- *"What really happens next?"*

- *"Does someone need to make a decision before this task?"*

- *"What approvals are required before proceeding?"*

- *"Is there anything missing in these tasks?"*

They first identified the input and output of the current process. Then, by focusing on the above questions, they began to identify the major tasks involved in carrying out Sure Strike's cash refund process. This time Rosa volunteered to record the following information on the flip chart:

Cash Refund Process For Returned Merchandise

PRODUCER: Accounts Payable Department

PROCESS: Cash Refund Process

INPUT: Returned Merchandise

OUTPUT: Refund Check

TASK #	MAJOR PROCESS TASKS	SUBTASKS/DECISIONS	SYMBOL
1	Customer Service receives returned merchandise		
1a		Company merchandise?	
1b		Merchandise returnable?	
1c		Return to sender	
2	Complete cash refund authorization form		
2a		Requires Accounting Manager approval?	
3	Forward completed form to Accounting Manager		
3a		Approved?	
4	Forward completed form to Accounts Payable		
4a		Form completed properly?	
5	Enter customer and refund data into computer system		
5a		Prepare weekly check run	
6	Print checks		
7	Review checks and verify amounts		
7a		Correct refund payment?	
8	Forward checks to Controller for signature		
8a		Check signed?	
9	Mail refund check to customer		
10	File Refund Authorization Form		

The team members thought they were familiar with the *Cash Refund Process*, but when they listed all the major tasks and decisions, they were amazed at how complex the process really was. *"I'm surprised it doesn't take a year for someone to receive a refund check!"* Althea remarked. Susan explained that the process actually took an average of ten working days. *"But we want to improve to meet our customers' expectations for refunds,"* she said, and everyone agreed.

B. Create a process flow chart

The second substep in documenting a process is to create a process flow chart. A flow chart is a step-by-step visual representation of the major tasks of a process.

Flow charts are helpful in a variety of ways, including:

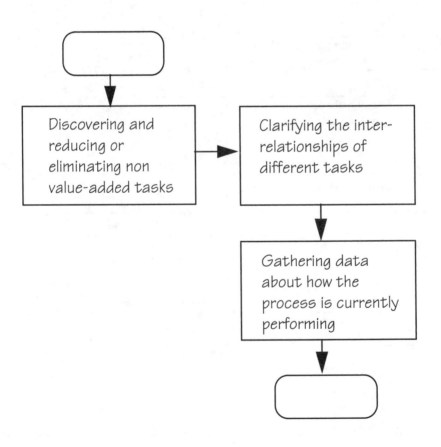

Listing tasks and drawing a flow chart are the first steps in analyzing a process. For easier analysis, it's important that you keep your list and flow chart simple. For example, if you are listing or flow charting the process tasks for preparing a written report, you wouldn't want to include every detail, such as:

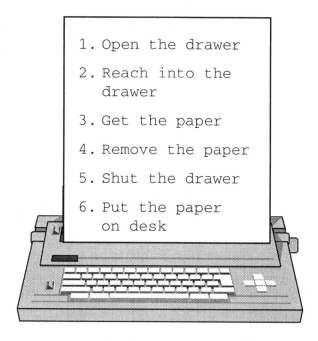

1. Open the drawer

2. Reach into the drawer

3. Get the paper

4. Remove the paper

5. Shut the drawer

6. Put the paper on desk

Too much detail defeats your purpose. You could end up with a flow chart big enough to wrap around an entire room. And the important process tasks would get lost in all that detail.

The Sure Strike team members decided to first review the symbols they'd be using in the flow chart. Some of the more common symbols used in flow charts include:

SYMBOL	NAME	EXPLANATION
	Elongated Circle	Shows the starting and ending points of a flow chart.
	Box	Any workflow task. Each box should contain a short description of the task being performed.
	Diamond	Any decision point. Each diamond should contain a question that can be answered "yes" or "no."
A	Connector	A small circle with a letter is used to connect one task of a flow chart to another.
	Document	A transfer (or output) of a hard copy document.
	Zigzag Arrow	Shows an electronic data transfer.
	Straight Arrow	Shows direction of process flow.

The team decided to draw the flow chart on the large flip chart pad. Kenji ended up drawing the flow chart that the team created. But prior to drawing it, the team members reviewed their list of major process tasks, subtasks, and decisions and added the symbol they would use for each item.

Task #	Major Process Tasks	Subtasks/Decisions	Symbol
1	Customer Service receives returned merchandise		
1a		Company merchandise?	
1b		Merchandise returnable?	
1c		Return to sender	
2	Complete cash refund authorization form		
2a		Requires Accounting Manager approval?	
3	Forward completed form to Accounting Manager		
3a		Approved?	
4	Forward completed form to Accounts Payable		
4a		Form completed properly?	
5	Enter customer and refund data into computer system		
5a		Prepare weekly check run	
6	Print checks		
7	Review checks and verify amounts		
7a		Correct refund payment?	
8	Forward checks to Controller for signature		
8a		Check signed?	
9	Mail refund check to customer		
10	File Refund Authorization Form		

Here's the flow chart they created for Sure Strike's *Cash Refund Process.*

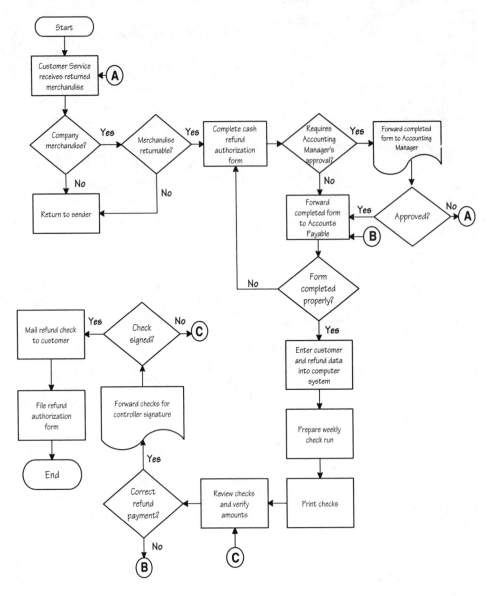

When they finished, they were pleased with what they'd produced. *"At first glance, this flow chart looks like a diagram for a circuit board on a rocket ship,"* Susan commented. *"But when you read it, it's a terrifically clear way to understand all the elements involved in the process."*

Identifying preliminary non value-added tasks

Prior to moving on to the second major step—Establish Process Measures, it's helpful to study your flow chart and discuss the value-added versus non value-added aspects of the process. Any non value-added tasks that you can identify at this point are usually opportunities for improvement.

Based on the complexity of the process flow chart, the Sure Strike team located areas in the process that appeared to be non value-added tasks that slowed down the process and/or didn't really add value to the desired output.

The two non value-added tasks they initially identified and listed on their flip chart were:

➠ Forward completed form to Accounting Manager—
The team felt that the Controller signing the check could also act as the approval.

➠ Enter customer and refund data into computer system —
The team felt that this information could be captured and entered by Customer Service.

Susan asked the team members to keep the cash refund tasks and the team's suggestions in mind as they continued working through the SAMIE Model.

4. Establish Process Measures

There is a saying in business that *"what gets measured, gets done."*
The cornerstone of process improvement is measurement. If you
measure process outputs and inputs, you'll be able to accurately
assess customer satisfaction and actually *"see"* the cause and effect
of solutions put into action.

Before you establish specific process measures, though, you must
decide what criteria you will use.

The Sure Strike team members knew that the ultimate goal of CPI is
to meet and/or exceed key customer requirements *(needs and
expectations).* Therefore, the team chose the customers'
requirements as the basis for determining which process measures
to use.

After some discussion, the team concluded that its process
measures must satisfy the following three major criteria:

> ➠ Linked to the customers'
> requirements—needs and
> expectations
>
> ➠ Measurable or countable—
> could be compared to
> acknowledged industry
> standard
>
> ➠ Observable—not a hidden
> measure that can't be
> tracked or compared

By using these criteria, the team felt confident it could establish process measures that would serve as objective, definable indicators to tell whether or not the process was delivering the outputs needed to meet or exceed Sure Strike's customer requirements.

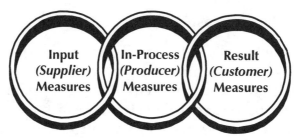

Types of measurements

There are three basic types of process measures: result *(customer)*, in-process *(producer)*, and input *(supplier)* measures.

Result measures

You can use result measures to judge the outcome of your process. They tell you how well your process has or has not met your customers' requirements. They are the same measures your customers are using to evaluate the effectiveness of your process.

Remember, *"customers"* is the key word here. You should establish measures to track and analyze what is important to your customers, not necessarily what is important to you and your organization. If you don't keep that in mind, you could waste time and energy tracking and analyzing the wrong things.

For example, if you are a pizza maker, your measure of the perfect pizza might be one where the pepperoni is arranged neatly on top of it without one piece touching another one. However, your customers' measure of the perfect pizza is a pizza that:

✓ They get quickly

✓ Is hot

✓ Has the right toppings

✓ Tastes good!

Your customers don't care whether or not the pepperoni is neatly displayed. If you're interested in customer satisfaction, you should be measuring and tracking only the four result measures that are important to your customers.

In-process (Producer) measures

In-process measures tell you how well your process is performing at certain critical points or milestones *within the process*. They enable you to determine just how effectively these points or milestones in the process contribute toward satisfying customer requirements. These measures keep your process in control.

Back to the pizza. You've learned that your customers' requirements are quick, hot, good-tasting pizza with the correct toppings. So, the in-process elements of your pizza-making process that you should be measuring are things such as:

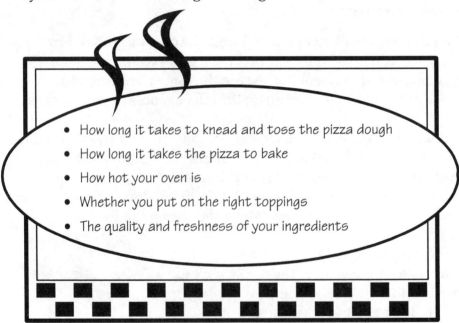

- How long it takes to knead and toss the pizza dough
- How long it takes the pizza to bake
- How hot your oven is
- Whether you put on the right toppings
- The quality and freshness of your ingredients

For instance, as you're tracking the accuracy of the toppings, if you notice you've accidentally put ham instead of pepperoni on the pizza, you can correct that mistake before you put the pizza in the oven *(and still meet your customers' requirements).*

In-process measures also make it possible for you to predict the future, and you don't even need a crystal ball. Let's say your boss is going to give a presentation and he or she needs a departmental report from you in two days. You know that it should only take two hours to get the research data you need to write the report. You also realize that the information gathering time has a potential lower limit of one hour and an upper limit of four hours.

Because you've previously measured the length of time it takes to gather information for a report, you know that you can finish the report on time. Even if the data gathering takes the maximum four hours in your time parameter, you can still do it. However, you would have to streamline some of the later tasks in the process to meet the overall process *"result measures."*

Input (Supplier) measures

Input measures help you assess how well suppliers are meeting your requirements. Input measures are typically established independently *(with each supplier to the process)*, since performance requirements may differ for each supplier.

Let's return to the pizza example. You, the pizza maker, are dependent on suppliers to provide you with quality supplies on a timely basis so you can fully satisfy your customers.

Depending on which supplier you're dealing with, you might need to measure quantity and quality of supplies, how often you receive them, and whether or not you've received the correct supplies. You'll establish independent measures with each supplier. For example, if you use fresh tomatoes, you'll need more frequent deliveries from that supplier than from your pizza box supplier. You'll also need to check the tomatoes more carefully to ascertain quality.

Determining result, in-process, and input measures

It is far better to have fewer meaningful measures than many ineffective measures. There are several traps you can fall into when measuring your processes.

✔ You can measure too many things.

✔ You can spend too much time measuring.

✔ You can measure the wrong things.

To determine result, in-process, and input measures for your processes, you must follow two steps for establishing each type of measure:

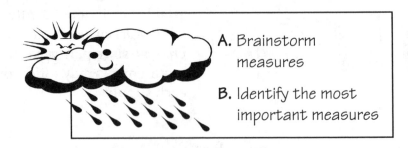

A. Brainstorm measures

B. Identify the most important measures

For result *(customer)* measures, use the information you gathered from your customer surveys and interviews. For in-process *(producer)* and input *(supplier)* measures, use the information on your flow chart.

After you've finished brainstorming, identify which of the measures you've brainstormed are most critical to your success. Revisit your customers and get agreement on result measures. Take the result measures and narrow down your list of in-process measures to those that have the greatest impact on your customer measures. Finally, look at your selected in-process measures. Then choose the input measures that will have the most impact on your performance, and get agreement with each supplier.

The Sure Strike team members reconfirmed their customers' most important requirements concerning the area of returns and exchanges. On the basis of all the data, the team determined that the Cash Refund Process needed to satisfy the following customer requirements:

- Refund mailed within 72 hours of receipt of returned merchandise

- Correct amount of money refunded in accordance with refund policy

- Receive follow-up confirmation of action being taken within 24 hours of receipt of returned merchandise if return will not be resolved within 72 hours

The team members believed that it currently took more than 72 hours to process a cash refund. Susan had told them that it took approximately ten working days. So they realized that one primary improvement opportunity was to reduce the time it took to get the refund to the customer and increase the efficiency of refund handling. In addition, they realized they didn't know how often customers received refund checks with the incorrect amount.

On the basis of these observations, as well as the specific customer requirements affecting this process, the team decided to track and analyze the following result measures:

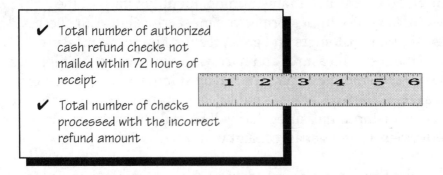

✔ Total number of authorized cash refund checks not mailed within 72 hours of receipt

✔ Total number of checks processed with the incorrect refund amount

Although the team knew it wanted to reduce the overall time it took for the Cash Refund Process, it was critical that the team make an informed decision prior to committing the company to a 72-hour turnaround for cash refunds. The team members knew they could not really determine a workable time frame for refunds until they understood how much time each process task was taking, and why.

The team also needed to establish the appropriate in-process measures on which to focus. Taking into account the result measures and customers' requirements, the team reviewed the process flow chart to identify the critical points or milestones that would have a major effect on achieving positive process results.

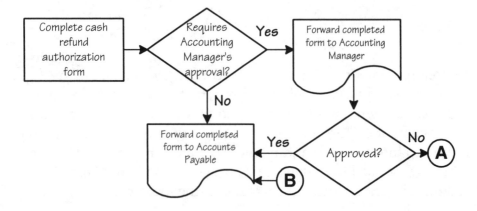

The team determined that two of the in-process measures to establish at this time included:

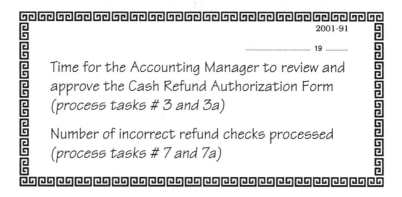

2001-91

_____ 19 _____

Time for the Accounting Manager to review and approve the Cash Refund Authorization Form (process tasks # 3 and 3a)

Number of incorrect refund checks processed (process tasks # 7 and 7a)

Finally, the Sure Strike team members took another look at the flow chart and chose the following two input *(supplier)* measures:

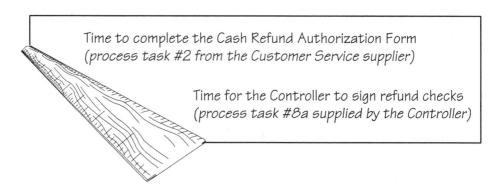

Time to complete the Cash Refund Authorization Form (process task #2 from the Customer Service supplier)

Time for the Controller to sign refund checks (process task #8a supplied by the Controller)

Both of these measures involved departments or individuals outside the Accounts Payable department, thus making them suppliers of services to the department.

During the next phase *(Measure)*, they could determine whether or not these in-process and input measures were the best ones to track and analyze on an ongoing basis.

Having documented the *"as is"* process and established process measures, it's time to move on to phase three, where you'll actually measure performance in your attempt to improve a process.

CHAPTER SIX WORKSHEET:
DOCUMENTING A PROCESS

1. List the major process tasks.

After you've selected a process to improve, make a list of the major process tasks, subtasks, and decisions that translate the suppliers' inputs into outputs that the process produces to satisfy customer requirements.

PRODUCER: _____

PROCESS: _____

INPUTS: _____

OUTPUTS: _____

TASK #	MAJOR PROCESS TASKS	SUBTASKS/DECISIONS	SYMBOL

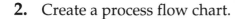

2. Create a process flow chart.

Referring to the process tasks, subtasks, and decisions you listed on the previous page, use the appropriate flow chart symbols to create a process flow chart for how the process currently works. (**Hint:** *When creating a process flow chart on the job, you may want to use sticky notes so you can make changes easily, then transfer it to a sheet of paper.*)

3. Review your flow chart.

Spend a few minutes reviewing your flow chart. Discuss your flow chart with others involved in the process. What feedback did you receive?

_____

_____

_____

4. In the space below, redraw your flow chart based on the feedback you have just received. For example, your revisions may include filling in who does what for each task, reworking the steps that are not clear, or making the arrows and boxes easier to understand.

5. What result, in-process, and input measures do you need to establish for the process?

KEY RESULT MEASURES	KEY IN-PROCESS MEASURES	KEY INPUT MEASURES

PHASE THREE: MEASURE

The Measure phase of CPI is vital. Measuring the process to establish an initial baseline performance level, and then continuing to measure the process, is the only way you can determine how well the process and major process tasks stack up against your customers' requirements.

Measuring the process involves the following two major steps:

5. Gather "baseline" performance data

6. Identify process performance "gaps"

5. Gather Baseline Process Performance Data

Gathering baseline performance data helps you see how effectively the process and the tasks within the process function to meet the requirements of your customers. Your picture of the process may be quite different from the actual process itself. The data you gather will clear up any discrepancies.

For the Sure Strike team, the timeliness *(or cycle time)* of the process and the accuracy *(correct amount)* were two of the most important requirements that customers had for the *Cash Refund Process*. On the basis of that information, the team decided to gather some baseline data.

To gather this data, the team decided to use Check Sheets. Check Sheets help track two important customer satisfaction indicators for the cash refund requests being processed during the next week. On the basis of past data, Susan estimated that approximately 25 to 30 cash refund requests were processed per week. Susan agreed to track the cycle time of the overall process. Rosa agreed to track the accuracy of the checks being processed. They presented the following data at the next team meeting.

Susan's Check Sheet

	MON 5/3/XX	TUES 5/4/XX	WED 5/5/XX	THURS 5/6/XX	FRI 5/7/XX	TOTAL
# PROCESSED	4	5	8	6	6	29
AVERAGE CYCLE TIME	99 hours (5 workdays)	92 hours (4 workdays)	116 hours (6 workdays)	102 hours (5 workdays)	105 hours (4 workdays)	103 hours (5 workdays)

Rosa's Check Sheet

	MON 5/3/XX	TUES 5/4/XX	WED 5/5/XX	THURS 5/6/XX	FRI 5/7/XX	TOTAL
# PROCESSED	4	5	8	6	6	29
# WITH INCORRECT AMOUNTS	0	1	3	1	0	5 (17% of total)

While it didn't take as long to process a check as Susan had thought, the process wasn't functioning at a level that would meet and/or exceed the customers' requirements. Susan suggested they use this preliminary data to begin identifying process problem areas. Then they could determine which performance *"gaps"* needed improvement.

6. Identify Process Performance "Gaps"

Process problem areas are responsible for causing gaps in meeting your customers' requirements. To close these performance gaps, you need to identify and solve problems *(e.g., eliminate non value-added tasks)* that may occur in each major task of a work process.

To help identify potential process performance gaps, the Sure Strike team chose to use a Problem Areas Matrix as a tool for finding some of those areas. If the team members could identify those gaps, they'd be able to focus their energies on how to close them. They would transform those gaps from problems into specific process improvement opportunities.

Utilizing a Problem Areas Matrix

The purpose of creating a Problem Areas Matrix is to narrow the scope of your analysis. It allows you to focus on improving specific areas of your value-added process. The matrix should be as simple as possible to adequately define process problem areas.

Larry volunteered to help the Sure Strike team create a Problem-Areas Matrix. He drew a diagram with enough space for the major tasks on the left and three to five problem areas along the top.

PROBLEM AREAS

MAJOR TASKS					
1.					
2.					
3.					
Etc.	Etc.	Etc.	Etc.	Etc.	Etc.

Although each process will have different potential problem areas, the following are common problem areas that you and your work group may encounter:

- ➤ Lack of clear procedures
- ➤ Takes too long
- ➤ Management not available
- ➤ Wasted resources
- ➤ Lack of training
- ➤ Poor communication
- ➤ Responsibilities unclear

Taking into account past process performance and/or feedback received from customers, the Sure Strike team brainstormed several possible problem areas and entered them in the spaces along the top of the matrix. Next, the team members compared each major task in the process against the listed problem areas and placed a check mark or "X" in each box for which the problem occurred.

PROBLEM AREAS

MAJOR TASKS	Lack of clear procedures	Management not available	Takes too long	Responsibilities unclear	MAJOR TASKS TOTALS	VALUE-ADDED TASK? (✔ if "Yes")
1. Customer Service receives returned merchandise				✗	1	✔
2. Complete cash refund authorization form				✗	1	
3. Forward completed form to Accounting Manager		✗	✗		2	
4. Forward completed form to Accounts Payable		✗			1	
5. Enter customer and refund data into computer system	✗		✗	✗	3	
6. Print cheques					0	✔
7. Review cheques and verify amounts		✗	✗	✗	3	
8. Forward cheques to Controller for signature		✗			1	✔
9. Mail refund cheque to customer					0	✔
10. File Refund Authorization Form					0	
PROBLEM AREAS TOTALS	1	4	3	4		

Problem Areas Matrix analysis

Once you've compared each major task to each problem area, total the scores and determine which of the tasks are value-added.

The Sure Strike team members formed the following initial conclusions based on the data provided in the matrix:

PROBLEM AREAS	MAJOR TASKS
Since *"management not available"* and *"responsibilities unclear"* were checked four times respectively, we need to take an approach that identifies clear responsibilities to improve our ability to complete each task in an efficient and timely manner.	Most of the problem areas checked occurred during major tasks #5 and #7 where *"someone enters data"* and then *"reviews data."* Improvement efforts should focus on these major tasks first.

Non Value-Added

The team also identified a number of non value-added tasks. Susan brought in an example of a refund authorization form that customer service representatives had to fill out every time a customer returned merchandise. The team members felt that the form required unnecessary information.

Once you've completed phase three, you can proceed to phase four, where you'll finally be able to devise and implement some initial improvement ideas.

CHAPTER SEVEN WORKSHEET:
PROCESS PROBLEM AREAS

1. Using a process you have selected, brainstorm three to five common problem areas which are affecting your ability to meet your customers' requirements.

Process: _____

Common problems with this process:

_____

_____

_____

2. Create a Problem Areas Matrix for the process you have selected. List the major tasks in the far left column. Summarize the problem areas for headings at the top of the matrix.

PROBLEM AREAS

MAJOR TASKS					MAJOR TASKS TOTALS	VALUE-ADDED TASK? (✔ if "Yes")
1.					___ ___	___
2.					___ ___	___
3.					___ ___	___
4.					___ ___	___
PROBLEM AREAS TOTALS	___	___	___	___		

3. List the two major tasks with the highest number of problem areas checked *(count left to right)*. How do these types of problem tasks impact performance for each of these two tasks?

PROBLEM TASKS	IMPACT ON PROCESS PERFORMANCE
Task with the highest number of problems:	
Task with the second-highest number of problems:	

4. List the two problem areas with the highest number of check marks. How do these types of problem areas impact process performance and create a *"gap"* in satisfying customer requirements?

PROBLEM AREAS	IMPACT ON PROCESS PERFORMANCE
Problem area with the highest number of checks:	
Problem area with the second-highest number of checks:	

5. List the *"non value-added"* process tasks which are creating *"gaps"* in the process's capability to produce an output which meets or exceeds the customers' requirements. Identify possible causes of the *"non value-added"* tasks.

NON VALUE-ADDED TASKS	POSSIBLE CAUSES

6. Using the information you have just completed, develop one or two preliminary improvement ideas for this process. What changes or actions might you and/or your work group take to begin improving the way this process performs?

a. _____

_____

b. _____

_____

c. _____

_____

d. _____

_____

PHASE FOUR: IMPROVE

In the previous three phases of the SAMIE model, you've had to do your homework. You've researched your customers' requirements to select a process, analyzed that process in detail, and measured its effectiveness. And while there's more work ahead, you'll actually see some of the fruits of your labor in this phase.

Improving your process involves the following two steps:

7. Set process improvement goal(s)

8. Develop and implement process improvements on a "trial-run" basis

These steps will ensure that your improvement efforts actually result in increased customer satisfaction.

7. Set Process Improvement Goal(s)

By definition, continuous improvement means that you are continually setting higher goals for yourself. In looking for ways to improve your processes, it is important to set improvement goals, meet them, and set new goals—continually improving on the way that your work is performed. It's a valuable habit to pick up.

Why set process improvement goals?

Why not just shoot for improvement in general? What purpose is there to setting specific goals for process improvement? The benefits of setting process improvement goals are hard to pass up.

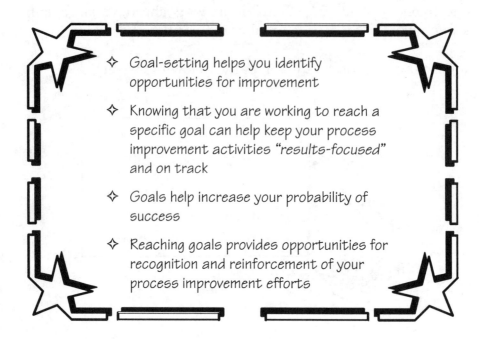

- ✧ Goal-setting helps you identify opportunities for improvement

- ✧ Knowing that you are working to reach a specific goal can help keep your process improvement activities "results-focused" and on track

- ✧ Goals help increase your probability of success

- ✧ Reaching goals provides opportunities for recognition and reinforcement of your process improvement efforts

If you're eager to realize the benefits of setting process improvement goals, follow these three substeps:

➠ Uncover improvement needs and opportunities

➠ Confirm desired process performance level on the basis of customer requirements

➠ Determine supplier performance requirements and specifications

Uncover improvement needs and opportunities

Now you need to analyze the performance gaps you identified in the previous phase. Put them under your customer satisfaction microscope and see if any glaring discrepancies come to light. Pick apart the major tasks of your selected process and pinpoint improvement opportunities. Once you've identified where specific improvements can be made, you can determine whether you'll be able to raise your performance level to meet or exceed your customers' requirements.

The Sure Strike improvement team had previously identified a number of gaps in performance that delayed the time it took for a customer to receive a cash refund. In particular, two tasks in the process took an inordinate amount of time. While other tasks could be streamlined, the team members decided to focus on these two improvement opportunities:

➡ The manager's review of the refund request and subsequent authorization,

➡ The accounting department's review of refund authorization and issuance of cheque request.

Confirming desired process performance level

You've uncovered opportunities for improvement. Now you need to know what goal to shoot for. That way you know in advance if your improvement effort will require a massive upheaval or only a minor reconstruction. Besides, once you know what your customers want, you can try to exceed their expectations to gain greater satisfaction.

You should review your
customer surveys. If necessary,
conduct additional interviews to
determine exactly what your
customers expect of you. For
example, you might discover
that when they call your
organization, they'll wait on
hold for two minutes, but three minutes is pushing it, and five
minutes has them fuming. Your goal is obvious: reduce time on
hold to two minutes or less.

The baseline performance data that Sure Strike's CPI team had
gathered revealed that it took Sure Strike an average of five
working days to complete the Cash Refund Process. And it took
the customers approximately ten days to two weeks to receive their
refund cheques. The customers felt that the current process took
much too long; one week was long enough to wait. That meant
Sure Strike definitely needed to streamline the Cash Refund
Process. If they could cut the time on their end to two or three
workdays, they'd be able to meet or exceed their customers'
expectations.

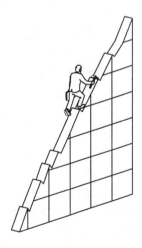

What your customers expect may not be
easily attainable, especially if the process
you're trying to improve hasn't changed for
years. If that's the case, it's advantageous to
set incremental goals. Set your primary goal
to reflect your customers' requirements, but
don't expect to reach that goal immediately.
Decide when you think it's feasible to reach
your major goal; then set reachable goals that
will lead to successful implementation of
your major goal.

Determining supplier performance requirements

Now that you've determined specific goals customers require, you're ready to meet with your suppliers to agree on desired performance levels *(goals)*. Reaching agreement on desired performance levels is important in developing successful Supplier-Producer-Customer relationships.

Make it your goal to become a partner with your suppliers. Perhaps most important is the realization that process improvement is a *"people event."* All change occurs through and with people. So you need to determine what changes you require of your suppliers. Only then can you sit down with them and discuss those changes.

Success in meeting customers' requirements is a win-win situation for both you and your suppliers, as long as current workloads and capabilities are taken into account. You may discover that a certain supplier can't fulfill your requirements or can only partially fulfill them. In that case, you'll have to go back to the drawing board and determine what needs to be done. Maybe you asked for too much.

The Sure Strike team members knew that they'd have to ask one of their suppliers, the customer service department, to make some changes and take on additional responsibilities. Since Susan was the customer service manager, she served as a sounding board for the team's ideas. *"If the Accounts department revises the authorization form to include only the information they need,"* she said, *"my department will be thrilled. They dislike filling out a page of information for one refund. But asking my department to enter the customer and refund data is pushing it. We're already working flat out."*

The team members discussed having a person help out in customer service for a couple of hours each day to enter the information or perhaps hiring an additional part-time customer service representative. Either way, they felt that the change in the process would help reduce the cycle time.

Setting process-improvement goals provides you with a specific destination. You know where you want to end up. You simply have to work through the maze to reach your goal by developing improvements that will head you in the right direction.

8. Develop And Implement Improvements On "Trial-Run" Basis

To develop improvements that will actually help you realize your process-improvement goals, utilize the observations you made and data you gathered in earlier phases. The key activities involved in developing and implementing process improvements on a trial-run basis include:

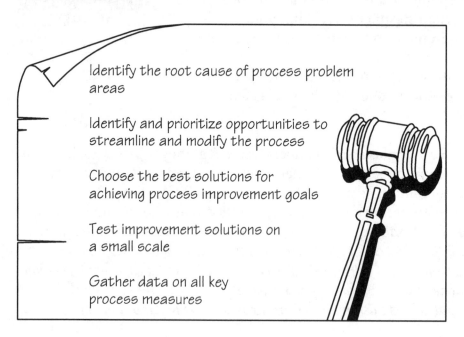

Identify the root cause of process problem areas

Identify and prioritize opportunities to streamline and modify the process

Choose the best solutions for achieving process improvement goals

Test improvement solutions on a small scale

Gather data on all key process measures

Identify the root cause of process problem areas

If you can identify the root cause of your process problem areas, you can target your improvement efforts accordingly. For example, if poor communication is one of your process problem areas, you need to identify why it is a problem. Is it because management has never encouraged open communication, because the office setup doesn't facilitate it, or because employees lack communication skills?

Brainstorm potential causes, determine the most likely causes, and finally identify the true root causes.

Note: There are a variety of continuous improvement tools designed to help you and your team at this and other stages of the CPI process. Refer to *Continuous Improvement Tools, Volumes 1 and 2*, for additional reference material.

The Sure Strike team came up with a list of what the team members considered to be potential causes for the time delays. They discovered that by using the Cause and Effect Diagram *(also known as the fishbone, or Ishikawa diagram)*, they were able to pinpoint potential causes more easily.

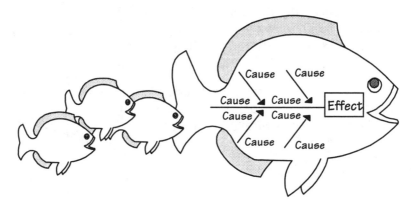

The box at the right end of the arrow *(the fish's head)* lists the timeliness problem area. That's known as the effect, or actual gap in the process, that the team wants to improve. The categories of potential causes that the team determined lead off the backbone of the fish.

To determine the most likely causes, interview the people who are intimately involved in the process you wish to improve. Share with them your list of potential causes; they'll tell you if you're on target or way off base. In fact, they may have ideas to add to your list.

Once you've identified the most likely causes, discuss each of them in detail. Ask questions, especially *"why"* questions. In so doing, you'll be able to get to the root cause or causes of your problem.

The Sure Strike team members held interviews with the individuals involved in the cash refund process in an effort to narrow down their list of potential causes. As a result, they were able to consolidate and trim their list. The team rated their top three likely causes in order:

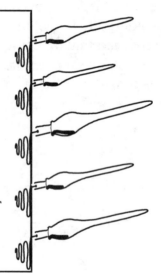

1. The manager was often unavailable to review and approve the refund request.

2. The accounting department had rigid schedules for issuing accounts payable cheques. They prepared customer refund cheques on Tuesdays and Thursdays only.

3. Too many signatures were needed on the refund cheque. The manager had to get the signatures of two company officers in addition to their own.

The Sure Strike team knew that all three of their most likely causes contributed to the timeliness problem. To reach their goal of cutting in half the time it took to receive a refund cheque, they decided to address these causes in the next six months.

Identify and prioritize opportunities to streamline and modify the process

Streamlining occurs when you redesign a process to be more efficient and to offer the least amount of resistance to the ultimate goal of that process. You can streamline by eliminating steps or by reducing the activities within the steps of a process. Modifying occurs when you make changes within a process so that it meets or exceeds your customers' requirements.

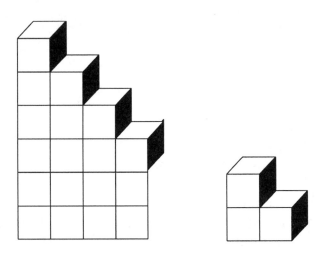

Up to this point, you've identified non value-added tasks you may be able to eliminate, and you've analyzed tasks within your process that you could modify. This is your chance to put all those ideas on the table and discuss whether they will actually help your improvement effort.

The Sure Strike team members listed their ideas on a flip chart. On one sheet, they identified the non value-added tasks that could be eliminated *(e.g., including unnecessary information on the authorization form)*. On another, they listed tasks within the cash refund process that they could modify for improvement *(e.g., requiring three signatures on each cheque)*. Then they rated the items on each list according to their improvement criteria.

Choose the best solutions for achieving process-improvement goals

Which solutions will achieve your goal of improvement? You have a choice to make as a team. You should have a number of ideas in front of you, but they aren't equally capable of producing the results you want. Keep in mind your criteria for improvement. If you don't have extra funds available for your improvement effort, hiring additional help might not be the way to go. Likewise, if you're limited on time, implementing an effort that requires many extra hours of training won't be the best solution.

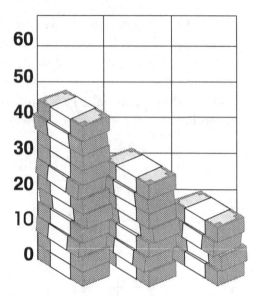

The Sure Strike team decided that eliminating non value-added tasks was an essential part of the solution. It wouldn't cost anything, and it would reduce the cycle time. The team members also decided that since the Accounting Manager wasn't always available to approve forms, the Assistant Manager could take over that task when needed. In addition, they determined it necessary to change the rigid schedule for preparing refund cheques. A specific person in the Accounting department would be designated to prepare the cheques daily.

Test improvement solutions on a small scale

Return to your original flow chart and modify it according to the changes you'll make. Cross out the processes you've eliminated and note the changes next to those you've modified. By doing this, you'll gain a clearer picture of how your changes will affect the process.

Then test your solutions. Don't make them *"standard operating procedure"* right away. Give your solutions a trial run and determine how well they work. If your results are positive, you'll have the go-ahead to implement your solutions.

The Sure Strike team started by trying out a few changes at a time. Susan met with her customer service department and reviewed the new form with them. The team met with the Accounting department, and clarified the changes to manager approval and the issuing of cheques. All of these changes were well-received.

Gather data on all key process measures

Here's where you'll gather the evidence that will either support your improvement efforts or sway you from continuing. Review the process measures you established in phase two and see if you need to add any in-process or input measures. Then gather enough data on each to allow you to make a decision whether or not to implement specific changes.

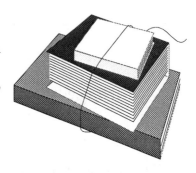

The Sure Strike team members tracked the average cycle time for refund cheques to determine whether this result measure had improved. They also formulated new in-process and input measures to reflect the new modifications to the cash refund process. Each team member volunteered to gather data on a different measure.

Once you've completed this phase of the SAMIE model, you'll have a pretty good feel for what continuous process improvement involves. The final phase will confirm whether your improvement efforts have hit their target or have at least come close.

CHAPTER EIGHT WORKSHEET: MAKING IMPROVEMENTS

1. List one of your work group's process improvement goals and any intermediate goals that you need to set to reach your primary goal. Include a time frame for each goal.

    Primary goal: _____

    _____

    We will reach this goal by: _____

    Intermediate goal #1: _____

    _____

    We will reach this goal by: _____

    Intermediate goal #2: _____

    _____

    We will reach this goal by: _____

    Intermediate goal #3: _____

    _____

    We will reach this goal by: _____

2. Choose one of your process problem areas.

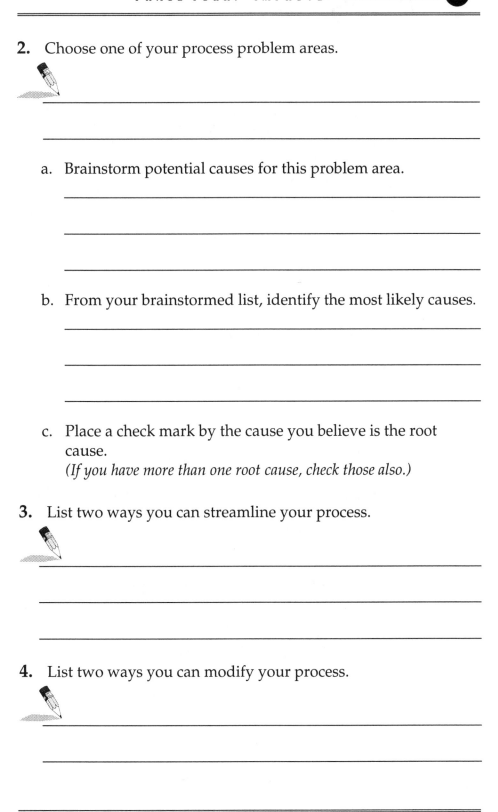

_____

_____

    a. Brainstorm potential causes for this problem area.

        _____

        _____

        _____

    b. From your brainstormed list, identify the most likely causes.

        _____

        _____

        _____

    c. Place a check mark by the cause you believe is the root cause.
        (If you have more than one root cause, check those also.)

3. List two ways you can streamline your process.

_____

_____

4. List two ways you can modify your process.

_____

_____

PHASE FIVE: EVALUATE

"Never take anything for granted."

Benjamin Disraeli

Your task isn't quite complete. You may have succeeded in finding solutions to the problem areas in your process. You may have even overhauled your process in your attempt to improve it. But you don't know whether or not your job was successful until you gather all the available feedback and data and evaluate it.

The Evaluate phase is composed of two major steps:

> **9.** Assess impact of process improvements
>
> **10.** Standardize process and monitor ongoing improvement

These steps focus on evaluating the effectiveness of the changes you have made to ultimately identify continuous improvement opportunities.

9. Assess Impact Of Process Improvements

This step will ensure that you determine whether or not your process improvements have reduced or eliminated the root cause(s) of your identified process problem areas. Following this step will help you determine whether your improvements have actually satisfied your customers' requirements.

Truly assessing the impact of process improvements requires that you:

➡ Solicit customer feedback during your trial-run period

➡ Review data related to your process improvement goals

➡ Determine if the root cause of process problem areas has been reduced or eliminated

➡ Verify that your improvements in process performance have been sustained

➡ Refine your improvements as needed

Solicit customer feedback during your trial-run period

The goal of CPI is to satisfy the customer, to ensure that processes meet or exceed customer requirements. Give your improvement effort the acid test: ask your customers! You may feel that your effort is successful, but if your customers feel otherwise, you haven't succeeded.

You may not have all the kinks ironed out during the trial-run period, but you should still see results. If not, you may have to go back to the drawing board. If customers sense improvement, then you're on the right track. You may still have to double your efforts, but at least you can see the light at the end of the tunnel.

The Sure Strike team members interviewed customers after they had implemented some improvements during the trial-run period. Since it was a rare customer that used their cash refund process on a regular basis (*how many bowling balls can you return in a year?*), the team members had to gauge the receptiveness of many customers new to the refund process. Their survey yielded less complaints, though, so they felt the improvements were working.

Reviewing, determining, and verifying

Remember the data you gathered in the previous phase? Here's where you put it to work. Data doesn't lie or cheat. Study it to determine whether your improvements have actually accomplished what you had hoped.

Next, determine if the root cause of your process problem areas has been reduced or eliminated. Let's return to a previous example. If one of your process problem areas is poor communication, and your work group found that the root cause was lack of communication skills, has your improvement effort taken care of that problem? Have communication skills improved?

The Sure Strike team reviewed the data the team members had gathered and found that it was taking less time for the cash refund process. Instead of taking an average of five workdays to complete the process, it only took four. The Accounting department had successfully changed the issuance of cheques from twice weekly to daily. But the time it took for the manager to approve the form was still too long. The team discovered that although the assistant manager was given the authority to approve the forms, she didn't consider it a high priority.

After you've reviewed the data and determined if the root cause has been reduced or eliminated, verify that your improvements to process performance have been sustained. Your improvements should last for more than one week.

Refine your improvements as needed

You're in luck if all of your implemented improvements achieve exactly what you hoped they would. You'd also be in a minority if that describes your CPI effort. More likely than not, you'll need to tweak some of your changes, redefine goals, or search for and eliminate additional non value-added tasks.

What was your conclusion when you determined whether your root cause had been reduced or eliminated? If you succeeded in eliminating it, congratulations! If it was reduced, was it to your satisfaction? Were you able to identify why you weren't able to eliminate the cause of your problem? Answering these questions will help you pinpoint where your improvements need refining.

The Sure Strike team members identified a potential problem in their implementation process when they discovered that a root cause had not been reduced. They thought that the accounting manager's unavailability could be rectified by giving the assistant manager the authority to approve refunds. But when the assistant manager let the authorization forms sit on her desk, one root cause was replaced with another. They talked with the assistant manager, explained the urgency of receiving her approval on the forms, and asked for her help. She agreed to take care of the approvals on a timely basis.

10. Standardize Process And Monitor Ongoing Improvement

By now, your initial improvement efforts have been successful or you've refined them so that you can reach your goals. But it's not over yet. You need to make sure that your improved process won't revert to the old way of doing things. To keep your process in top form, you have to standardize it and monitor its ongoing improvement. Only then will your changes be successful.

This last step in the CPI process involves the following key activities:

- Communicate improved process flow and operating guidelines

- Conduct training on improved process as needed

- Gather and provide ongoing customer and supplier feedback

- Hold and continually improve process performance gains

- Disband process improvement team as needed

Communicate improved process flow and operating guidelines

Part of standardizing your improved process is incorporating it into your organization's procedures. Whether that involves including it in an organizational manual or handing out a list of the new operating guidelines, your revised process should be more than just a verbal agreement between current producers and suppliers. Otherwise, you'll be in trouble if you have a major employee turnover or your current suppliers take a vacation.

It's also important to communicate what you've accomplished to your entire organization. It will not only ensure that your producers and suppliers stay on top of the process (*since everyone will be watching*), but it will also serve as positive reinforcement. It might even encourage other departments to undertake their own CPI efforts.

The Sure Strike team met with all of the individuals involved in the cash refund process. The team members distributed a copy of the revised flow chart and a list of the new operating guidelines. The different departments could easily see how they contributed to the improvements. Rosa and Mark gave a presentation to top management, sharing information about the improvements that had been implemented and their results. The managers were impressed; they asked Rosa and Mark to keep them informed on the progression of their improvement effort.

Conduct training on improved process as needed

Not everyone picks up on changes easily. You can't assume that a complicated change will be successfully implemented on the first go-around. That's why you must monitor your improvements and provide additional training, if necessary. Only then will you be able to reach your goals.

The Sure Strike team discovered the importance of this activity when it implemented the change of having customer service personnel input information into the computer system. The Accounting department had previously completed this task. Some customer service representatives forgot this step when they were busy; others completed it incorrectly. Susan held an additional training session for her representatives and double-checked the procedure daily.

Gather and provide ongoing customer and supplier feedback

It's feedback that fuels the effectiveness of any process changes. Gathering customer feedback allows you to gauge how you are doing and whether your changes are targeted correctly. You won't be making decisions in a vacuum.

Gathering feedback from your suppliers is also critical. They can let you know if your demands are within reason. Providing feedback to your suppliers also allows them to make additional changes to please you *(if your feedback suggests correction)* or gives them the motivation to work harder for you *(if your feedback is positive)*. You should make gathering and providing feedback an integral part of your improvement effort.

The Sure Strike team members knew that feedback was important to their success. On a regular basis, they called customers who had recently received refunds. The customer feedback did reflect that the improvements Sure Strike implemented were working, although they were still short of reaching total customer satisfaction. After experiencing the difficulty with customer service representatives learning to input information into the computer, the team kept close tabs on them. It wasn't long before the customer service representatives mastered the new procedure, and the team members let them know they were pleased.

Hold and continually improve process performance gains

Standardizing your process and monitoring its ongoing improvement will keep you in close touch with your process. That's the only way you'll be able to reach your goal of performing your process in the best way possible. By now, you've established intermediate goals that serve as *"performance milestones"* along the way to achieving your objectives. You should continually strive to reach the next milestone until you attain your ultimate goal.

The Sure Strike team reached its initial intermediate, or incremental, goal of cutting one workday off the time cycle of the cash refund process. The next two months found the team members at their second milestone—reducing the time cycle by an additional day. Now they had to really work to reach their final goal—reducing the cycle by one more day, which would cut the time of their original cycle in half. To do so, they would have to streamline the process further. It wouldn't be easy, but they were committed to doing it.

Disband process improvement team as needed

If your CPI team was formed to improve a specific task, you'll have to decide when to disband it. Will it be when you have reached your ultimate goal? Or perhaps you'll wait until you are assured that you'll continue to meet that goal. Or you might want to keep your team together to take on other processes that need improvement.

It's your call. If this is the first time you've ever formed a CPI team and the members did a great job, think about having them discuss their process with the organization or even have them train managers to successfully improve processes within their own departments. CPI isn't meant to be a start-and-stop venture. It's a way of life.

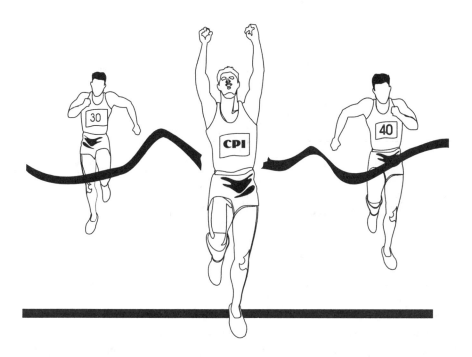

CHAPTER NINE WORKSHEET:
ASSESSING IMPROVEMENT IMPACTS

For one of your primary customers, identify a key process and one or two outputs that you produce. Use the worksheet below to document your progress to date. Remember, when it comes to your continuous process improvement efforts, all measurable improvements are important!

Producer: _____ Process: _____

Customers: _____

Suppliers: _____

My/Our Output	Customer Requirements (Desired Performance)	Initial "Baseline" Performance Level	Improvements Made To The Process	Current Performance Level	Impact Of Improvement Efforts

Now analyze your assessment by responding to the following questions. This will help you examine your perceptions of the impact and progress of your initial improvement efforts.

1. How well did my process improvement efforts help me to better meet my customers' requirements?

   _____

   _____

   _____

2. What can I do to involve my suppliers in developing and implementing process improvement ideas?

   _____

   _____

   _____

3. What else do I need to know to be able to evaluate the effectiveness of my improvement efforts?

   _____

   _____

   _____

4. What other changes should I make to the process to help me meet my customers' requirements?

   _____

   _____

   _____

   _____

CHAPTER TEN

SUMMARY

As your business continues to grow and change, it's important to maintain it carefully. It's possible that some of the work processes that worked well one or two years ago may not be the most effective or productive processes to use if you hope to meet current and future quality demands. The stakes are high and the challenge is clear: you must continue improving to remain competitive!

Continuous process improvement is imperative for success. In today's competitive arena, CPI will take you to the major leagues. By improving processes, you improve results. And improving results means that you're on your way to reaching top performance.

CPI techniques will also help you discover new opportunities. Instead of having to react to problems that plague organizations that resist change, CPI allows you to act on possibilities that you uncover as you attempt to improve. Since one improvement leads to another, you'll quickly increase customer satisfaction. There's no downside to CPI.

The SAMIE model, charts, and worksheets included in this guidebook will give you the tools and the focus to begin your improvement efforts. Both you and your organization can build quality and success by continually improving processes.

Give it a chance. Once you realize what CPI can do for you and your company, you won't give it up. It's a habit-forming endeavor that will transform your organization!

INTERVIEWING YOUR CUSTOMER

Before you can identify potential work process improvements, it is critical to thoroughly understand how you are currently performing for your customers.

Using the sample questions provided below and any additional questions you feel would be appropriate, interview your top priority customers on the job. Record specific notes concerning your customers' requirements, and any agreements that may impact your producer-customer relationship.

Producer/Work Group Name _____

Interviewer(s) _____

Customer _____ **Date** _____

---

1. What products/services do you need from me to do your job effectively?

_____

_____

2. What are the requirements *(needs and expectations)* for each of these products/services?

PROCESS	PRODUCTS/SERVICES	REQUIREMENTS *(Needs and Expectations)*
A.		
B.		
C.		
D.		

3. Why do you depend on me to provide these products/services to you?

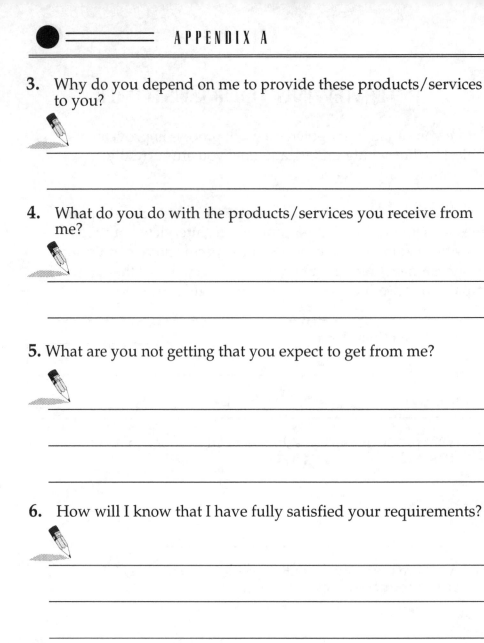

_____

_____

4. What do you do with the products/services you receive from me?

_____

_____

5. What are you not getting that you expect to get from me?

_____

_____

_____

6. How will I know that I have fully satisfied your requirements?

_____

_____

_____

7. How will I know that I have not fully satisfied your requirements?

_____

_____

_____

8. Is there anything that I'm providing to you that you no longer need or expect to receive from me?

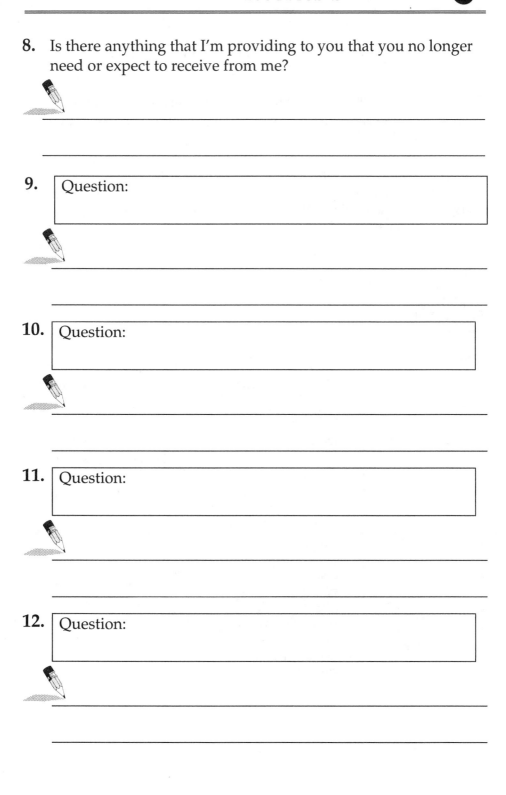

9. | Question: |

10. | Question: |

11. | Question: |

12. | Question: |

APPLYING THE SAMIE MODEL

The following table outlines the SAMIE phases, their major steps, the key activities, and some of the possible methods or tools that you may use.

Note: The possible method listed below may be helpful for you or your Process Improvement Team during various steps. Refer to the Continuous Improvement Tools Volume 1 and 2 guidebooks for additional reference on how to apply many of these methods and tools.

PHASE: SELECT

	KEY ACTIVITIES	METHODS/TOOLS
1. Define key requirements for "core" customers	• Form process improvement team • Identify your customers • Conduct customer needs assessment • Determine most critical output requirements *(needs and expectations)*	• Team formation guidelines • Team selection matrix • Customer assessment survey • Interviewing
2. Determine process to improve	• List processes that produce output for customer • Establish process selection criteria • Choose highest priority process needing improvement based on customer requirements	• Brainstorming • Multivoting • Process selection criteria • Selection matrix • List reduction

PHASE: ANALYZE

	KEY ACTIVITIES	METHODS/TOOLS
3. Document "as is" process	• Define process boundaries • Clarify *"process chain"* • Create flow chart of current process • Identify value-added and non value-added tasks	• Interviewing • Major process tasks list • Process flow chart • Tree Diagram
4. Establish process measures	• Establish *"input" (supplier)*, *"in-process" (producer)*, and *"result" (customer)* measures • Identify the most important measures to track	• Brainstorming • Interviewing • List reduction

PHASE: MEASURE

	KEY ACTIVITIES	METHODS/TOOLS
5. Gather *"baseline"* process performance data	• Collect quantitative performance data related to customer requirements • Establish feedback methods • Document findings and continue collecting quantitative data ongoing	• Check Sheet • Run Chart • Histogram • Scatter Diagram • Control Chart
6. Identify process performance *"gaps"*	• Compare current process data to customer requirements • Uncover known *"gaps"* in meeting customer requirements • Determine chronic process problem areas	• Gap analysis worksheet • Problem areas matrix • Process flow chart • Interviewing • Pareto Chart

PHASE: IMPROVE

	KEY ACTIVITIES	METHODS/TOOLS
7. Set process improvement goals	• Determine true process performance *"gaps"* in meeting customer requirements • Uncover improvement needs and opportunities • Confirm desired process performance level based on customer requirements • Determine supplier performance requirements and specifications	• Process flow chart • Brainstorming • Goal setting • Multivoting • List reduction • Customer and supplier negotiation • Criteria rating form
8. Develop and implement process improvements on a trial-run basis	• Identify *"root cause"* of process problem areas • Identify and prioritize opportunities to streamline and/or modify the process • Choose best options for achieving process improvement goals • Test improvements on a small scale • Operate process according to test plan • Gather quantitative data on all key process measures • Solicit customer feedback during *"trial run"* period	• Cause and Effect Diagram • Force field analysis • Affinity Diagram • Process decision program chart • Criteria rating form • Action plan • Process flow chart • Check Sheet • Run Chart • Control Chart

PHASE: EVALUATE

	KEY ACTIVITIES	METHODS/TOOLS
9. Assess impact of process improvements	• Review quantitative data related to process improvement goals • Determine if root cause of process problem areas has been reduced or eliminated • Verify that improvements in process performance have been sustained systematically rather than ad hoc occurrences • Refine improvements as needed	• Interviewing • Customer feedback survey • Evaluation assessment • Process flow chart • Action plan
10. Standardize the process and monitor ongoing improvement	• Communicate improved process flow and operating guidelines • Conduct training on improved process as needed • Gather and provide ongoing customer and supplier feedback • Hold and continually improve process performance gains • Disband process improvement team as needed	• Interviewing • Customer feedback survey • Evaluation assessment • Process flow chart • Supplier certification • Benchmarking • Team summary report

THE PRACTICAL GUIDEBOOK COLLECTION

QUALITY IMPROVEMENT SERIES

- Meetings That Work!
- Continuous Improvement Tools Volume 1
- Continuous Improvement Tools Volume 2
- Step-By-Step Problem Solving
- Satisfying Internal Customers First!
- Continuous Process Improvement
- Improving Through Benchmarking
- Succeeding As A Self-Managed Team
- Reengineering In Action

MANAGEMENT SKILLS SERIES

- Coaching Through Effective Feedback
- Expanding Leadership Impact
- Mastering Change Management
- Effective Induction And Training
- Re-Creating Teams During Transitions

HIGH PERFORMANCE TEAM SERIES

- Success Through Teamwork
- Team Decision-Making Techniques
- Measuring Team Performance
- Building A Dynamic Team

HIGH-IMPACT TRAINING SERIES

- Creating High-Impact Training
- Identifying Targeted Training Needs
- Mapping A Winning Training Approach
- Producing High-Impact Learning Tools
- Applying Successful Training Techniques
- Measuring The Impact Of Training
- Make Your Training Results Last

EVALUATION AND FEEDBACK FORM

We need your help to continuously improve the quality of the resources provided through the Richard Chang Associates, Inc., Publications Division. We would greatly appreciate your input and suggestions regarding this particular guidebook, as well as future guidebook interests.

Please photocopy this form before completing it, since other readers may use this guidebook. Thank you in advance for your feedback.

Guidebook Title: _____

1. Overall, how would you rate your *level of satisfaction* with this guidebook? Please circle your response.

   Extremely Dissatisfied   Satisfied   Extremely Satisfied

   1   2   3   4   5

2. What specific *concepts or methods* did you find <u>most</u> helpful?

   _____

   _____

3. What specific *concepts or methods* did you find <u>least</u> helpful?

   _____

   _____

4. As an individual who may purchase additional guidebooks in the future, what *characteristics/features/benefits* are most important to you in making a decision to purchase a guidebook *(or another similar book)*?

   _____

   _____

5. What additional *subject matter/topic areas* would you like to see addressed in future guidebooks?

   _____

   _____

Name *(optional):*

Address: _____

C/S/Z: _____ **Phone (   )** _____

PLEASE FAX YOUR RESPONSES TO: (714) 756-0853   USA
OR (0171) 837-6348 UK